AF231251

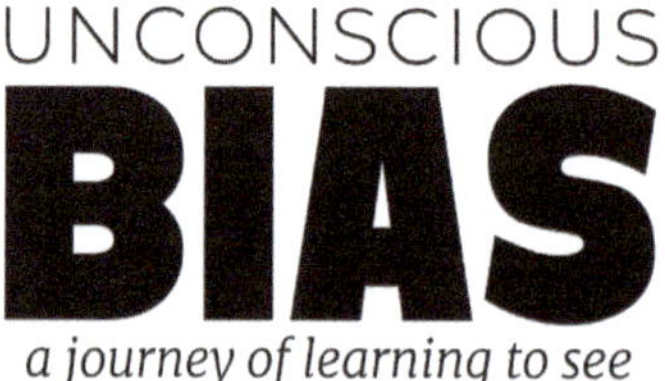

a journey of learning to see

———

ISBN: 978-0-9997601-9-2

Street Photography
Samuel Lee | slwe@me.com

Design & Layout
Tim B. Gilman | timmyroland.com

———

Common Good Coalition
cgcoalition.com

To all those that know that they don't know
but desire to understand . . .

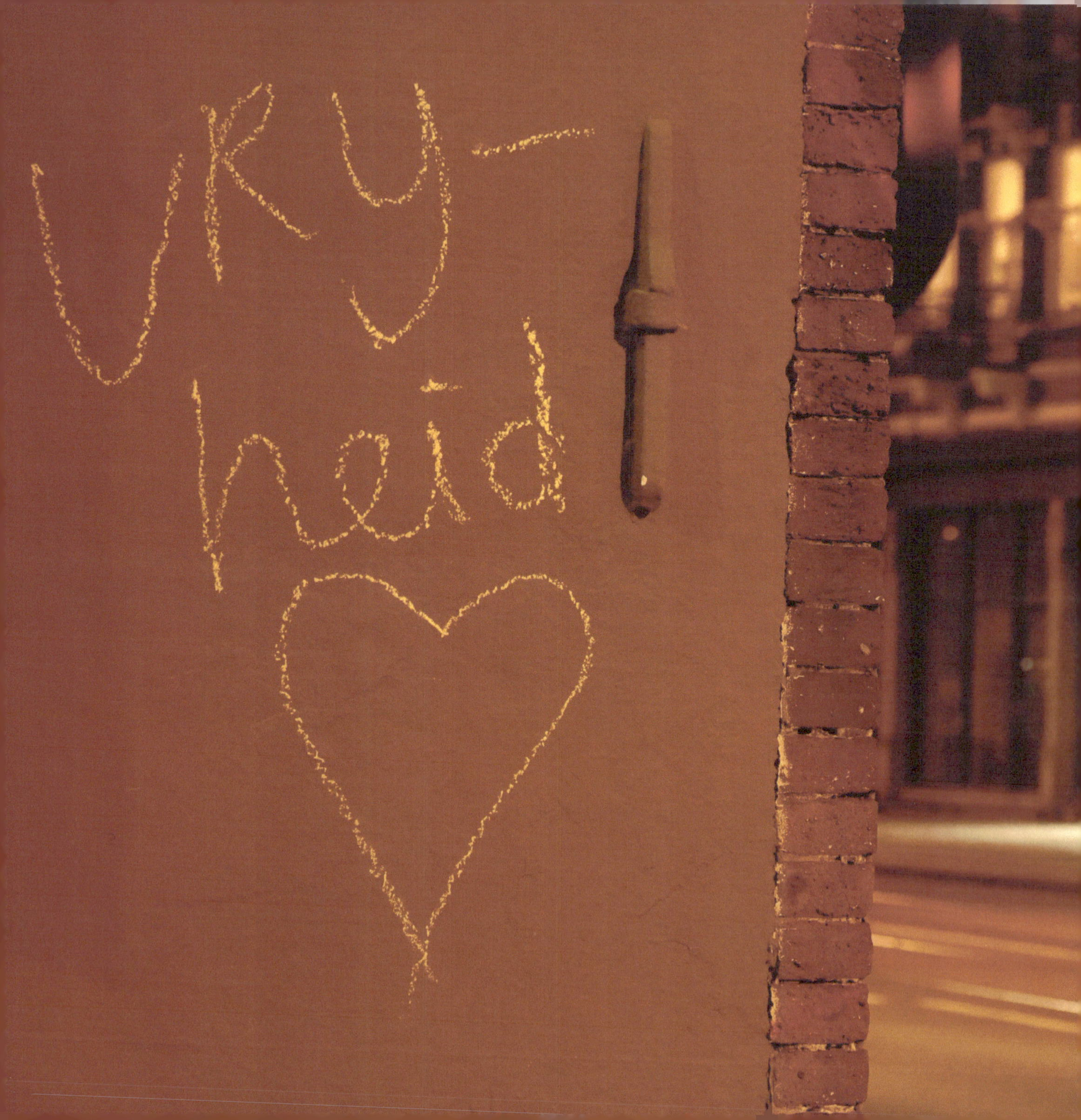
vry-
heid

My inability to act is always a reflection of my inability to love.

Fr. Richard Rohr

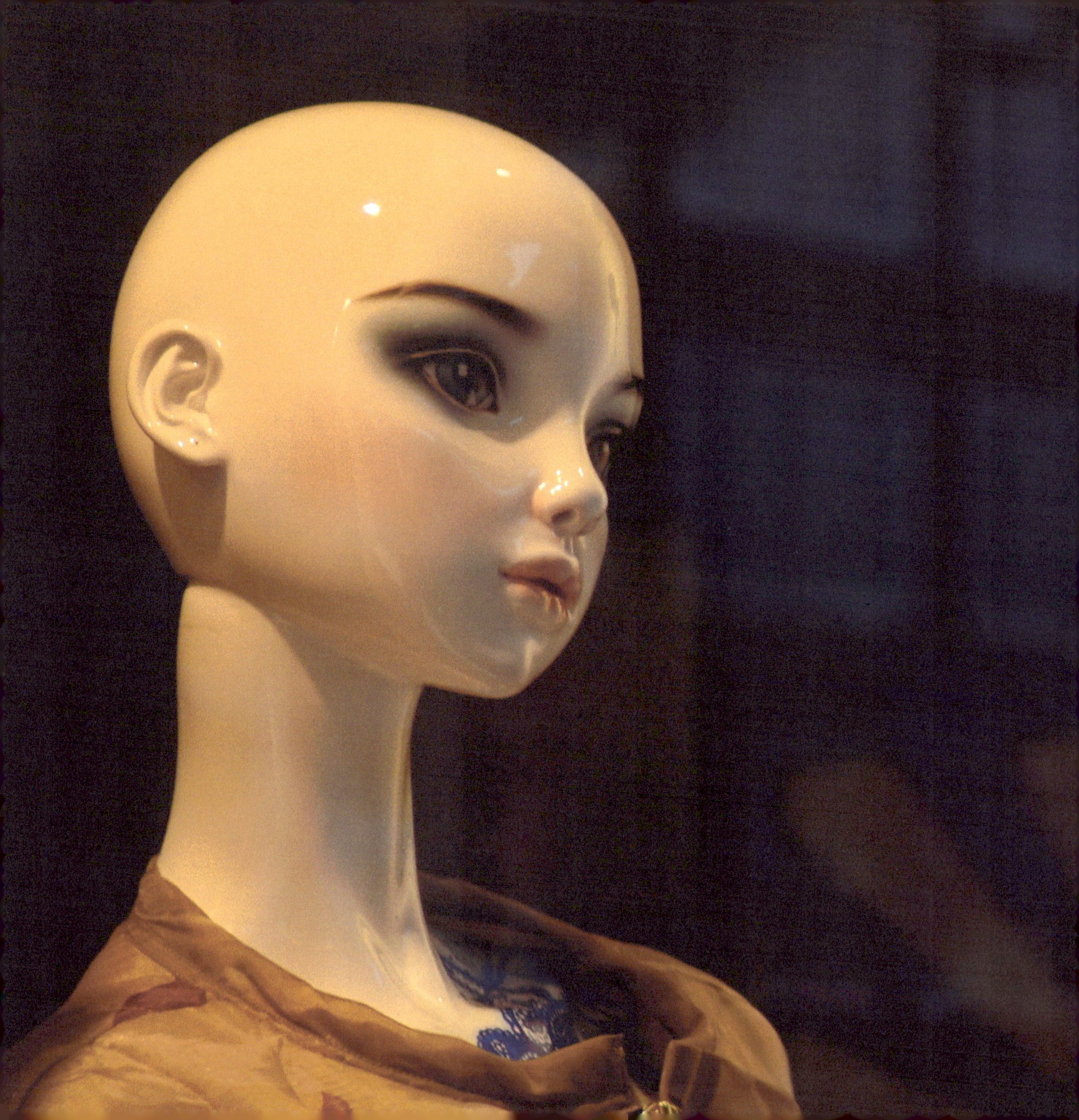

Preface

When I began researching the subject of bias, I was simply trying to make sense of some disturbing things I saw happening around me in the political and religious worlds. I had no idea that my research would turn into an extended essay in the form of a short e-book *"Why Don't They Get It? Overcoming Bias in Others - and Yourself"*. Nor did I expect that that extended essay would inspire a podcast, *"Learning How to See"*, co-hosted with my dear friends and colleagues **Fr. Richard Rohr** & **Rev. Dr. Jacqui Lewis.** And never in my wildest dreams could I have guessed that Tim Gilman, Creative Director for the **Common Good Coalition** would invite me to team up with our mutual friend **Rev. Dr. Samual Lee**, who, in addition to his extraordinary leadership in a congregation and university, is also an artist with a deep love of photography.

The idea for this book is simple: As you reflect on each of the thirteen biases we'll cover, you'll find a photograph to savor. Let its composition and colors still you and then move you, and then start writing. You might write a prayer or a poem. You might tell a story. You might jot down some spontaneous reactions, or even a list of questions for further consideration.

One of my mentors says, "Learning is not the consequence of teaching." (Or, I might add, writing and reading or listening to a podcast.) "Learning is the consequence of thinking," he says. So, we offer you this book to assist you in thinking . . . thinking as you slow down and sit in quiet reflection . . . thinking as you write . . . thinking as you reflect on what you write.

In many ways, biases are shortcuts around thinking. They are ways our brains try to say, "You're busy enough already. No need to think about this." Shortcuts are sometimes helpful, but sometimes, they lead to dangerous dead ends.

Thanks for your interest. Thanks for thinking, and learning!

Brian

Brian D. McLaren
May 2021

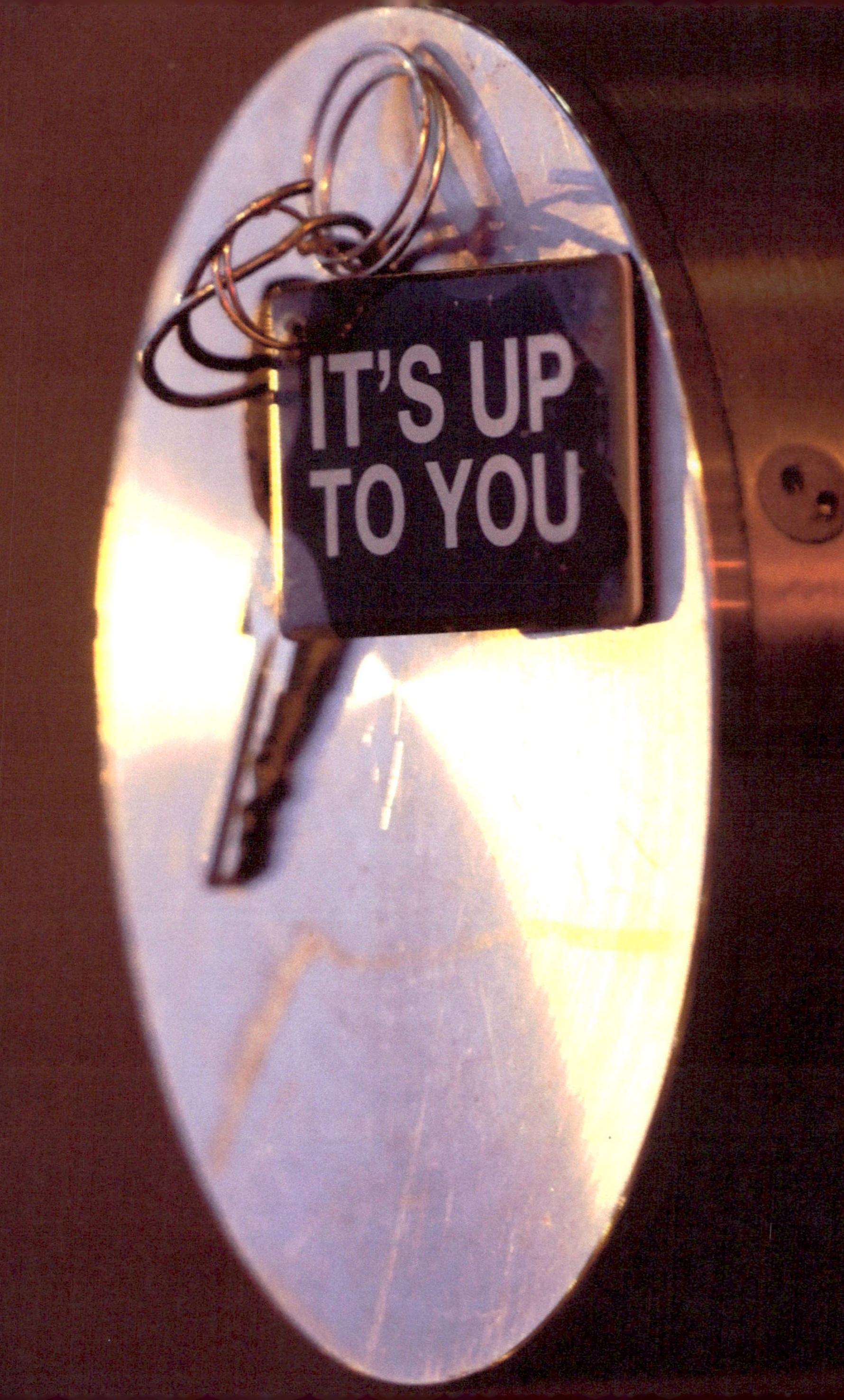
IT'S UP
TO YOU

UNCONSCIOUS
BIAS

a journey of learning to see

Brian D. McLaren
& Samuel Lee

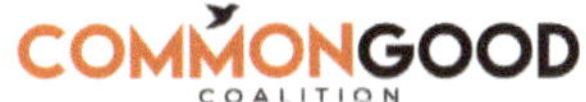

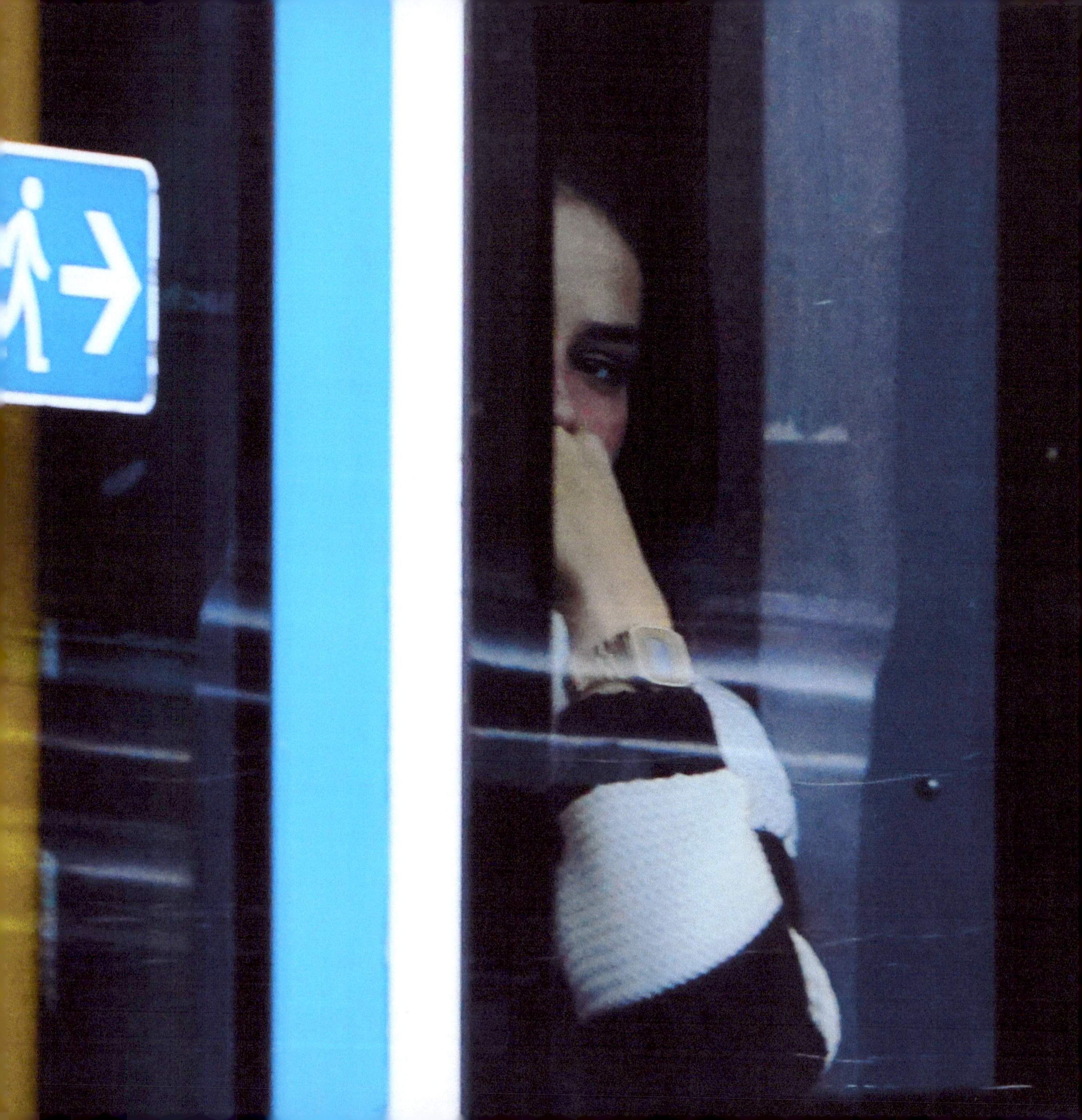

Confirmation

★ ★ ★

The human brain welcomes information that confirms what it already thinks and resists information that disturbs or contradicts what it already thinks.

....

....

....

....

....

....

....

Prayer & Contemplation

Source of all truth, help me to hunger for truth, even if it upsets, modifies, or overturns what I already think is true. Guide me into all the truth I can bear, and stretch me to bear more, so that I may always choose the whole truth—even with disruption—over half-truths with self-deception. Grant me passion to follow wisdom wherever it leads.

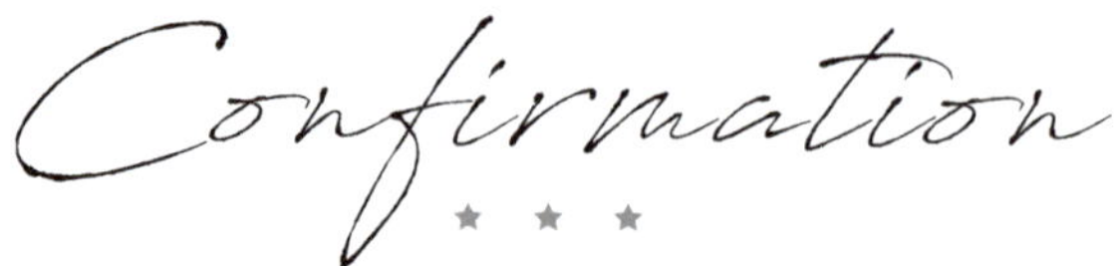

Confirmation

★ ★ ★

The human brain welcomes information that confirms what it already thinks and resists information that disturbs or contradicts what it already thinks.

Confirmation

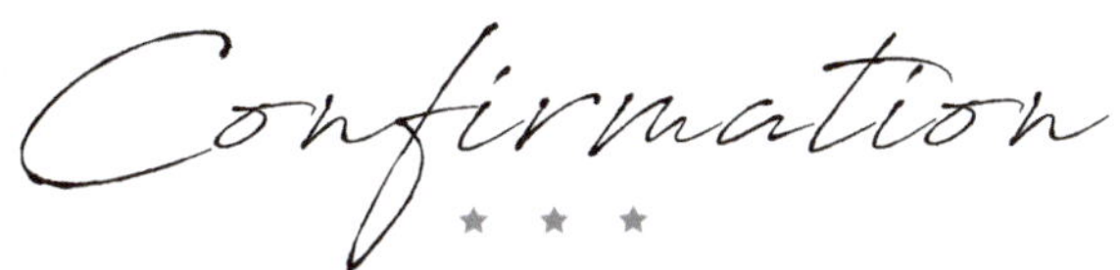

The human brain welcomes information that confirms what it already
thinks and resists information that disturbs or contradicts what it already thinks.

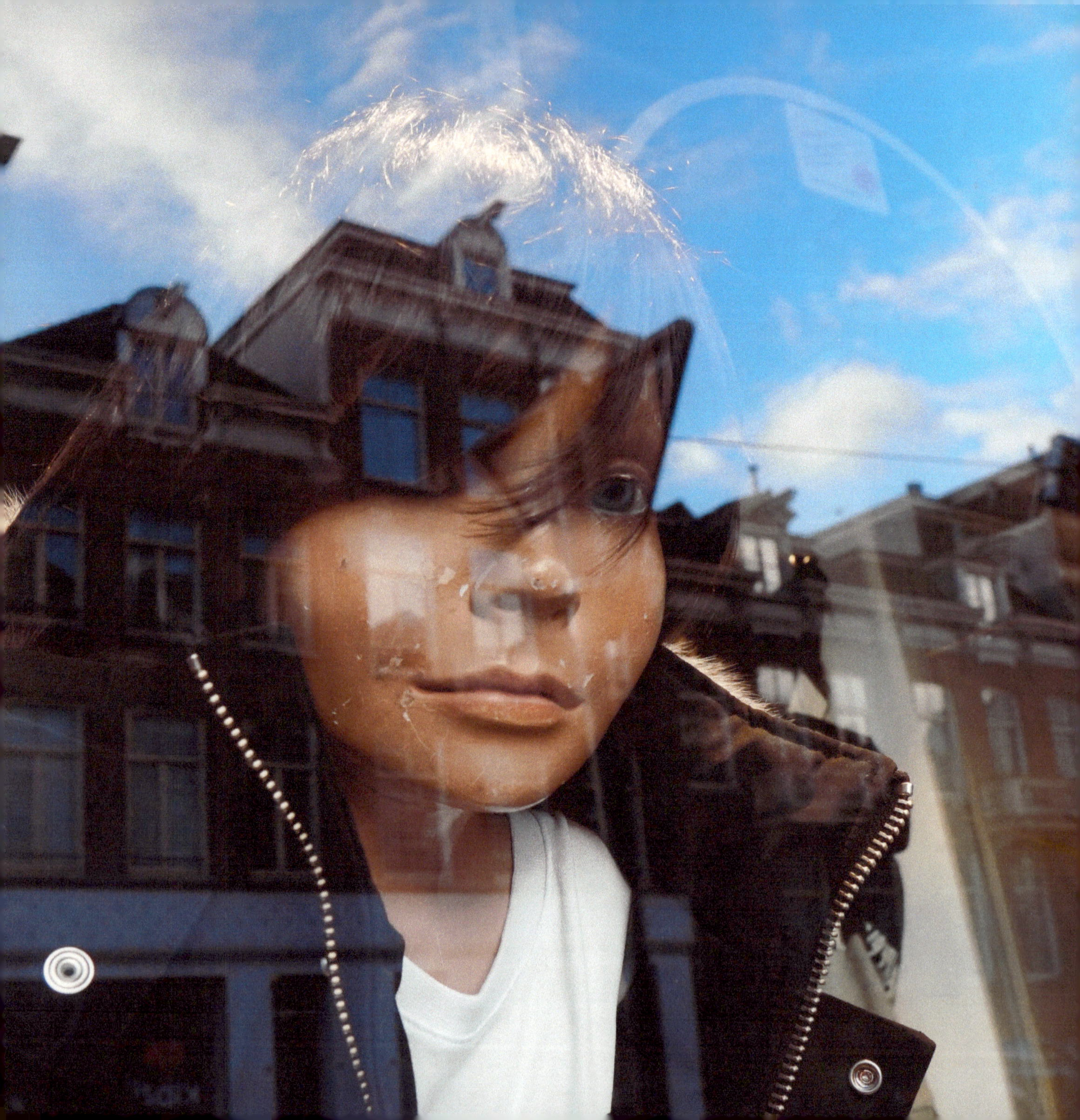

Complexity

★ ★ ★

The human brain prefers a simple lie to a complex truth.

....

....

....

....

....

....

....

....

Prayer & Contemplation

Spirit of wisdom and understanding, help me not be seduced by simple lies or repelled by complex truths. Instead, teach me to seek out understanding as if it were hidden treasure, digging deep beneath surface appearances to discover what is real in the depths.

Complexity

★ ★ ★

The human brain prefers a simple lie to a complex truth.

Complexity

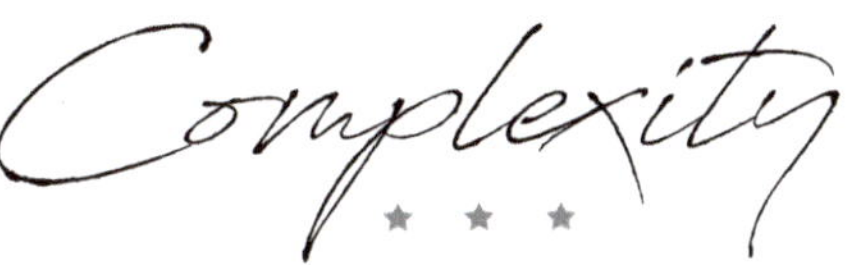

* ★ ★ ★ *

The human brain prefers a simple lie to a complex truth.

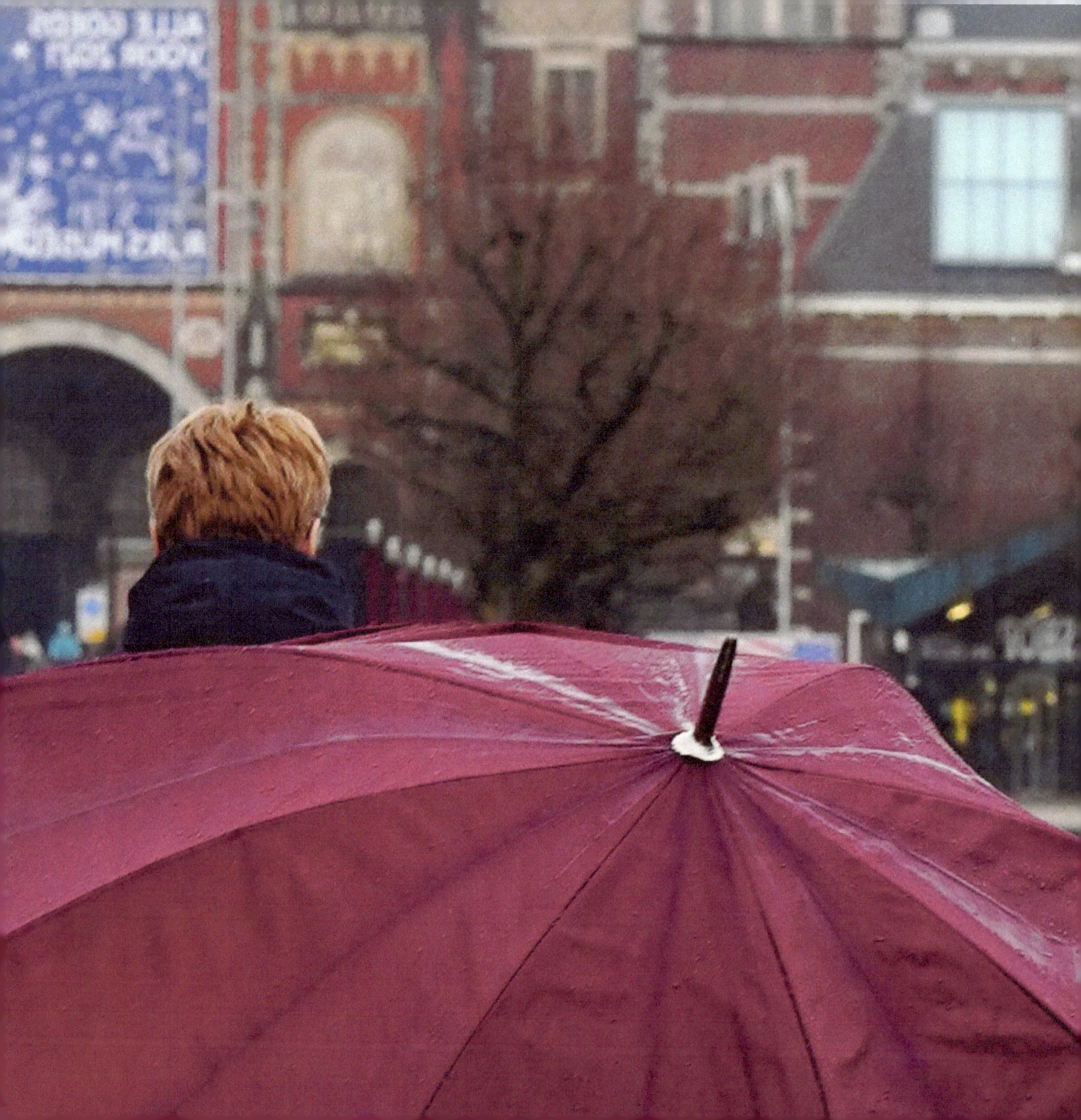

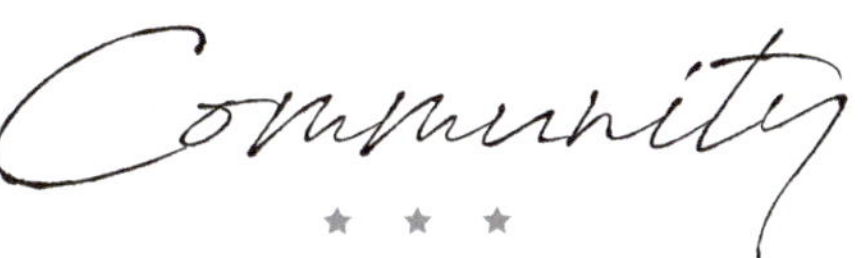

Community

★ ★ ★

The human brain finds it very hard for you to see something your group
doesn't want you to see. Also known as social confirmation bias, this bias puts tribe over truth.

....

....

....

....

....

....

....

....

Prayer & Contemplation

Inspirer of holy boldness and humble bravery, give me the humility to learn from my community whenever I can, along with the courage differ graciously from my community whenever I must. Help me seek truth even when my companions are unwilling to see it or accept it. Help me remain humbly loyal to the truth even when I am misjudged and rejected by my community for doing so.

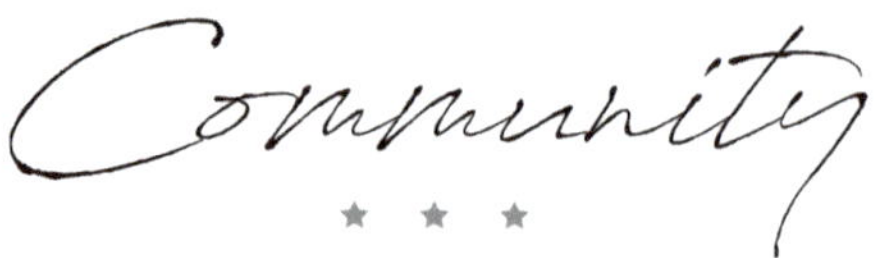

The human brain finds it very hard for you to see something your group
doesn't want you to see. Also known as social confirmation bias, this bias puts tribe over truth.

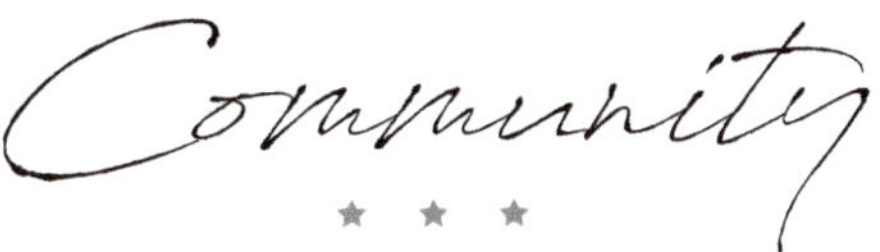

Community

★ ★ ★

The human brain finds it very hard for you to see something your group doesn't want you to see. Also known as social confirmation bias, this bias puts tribe over truth.

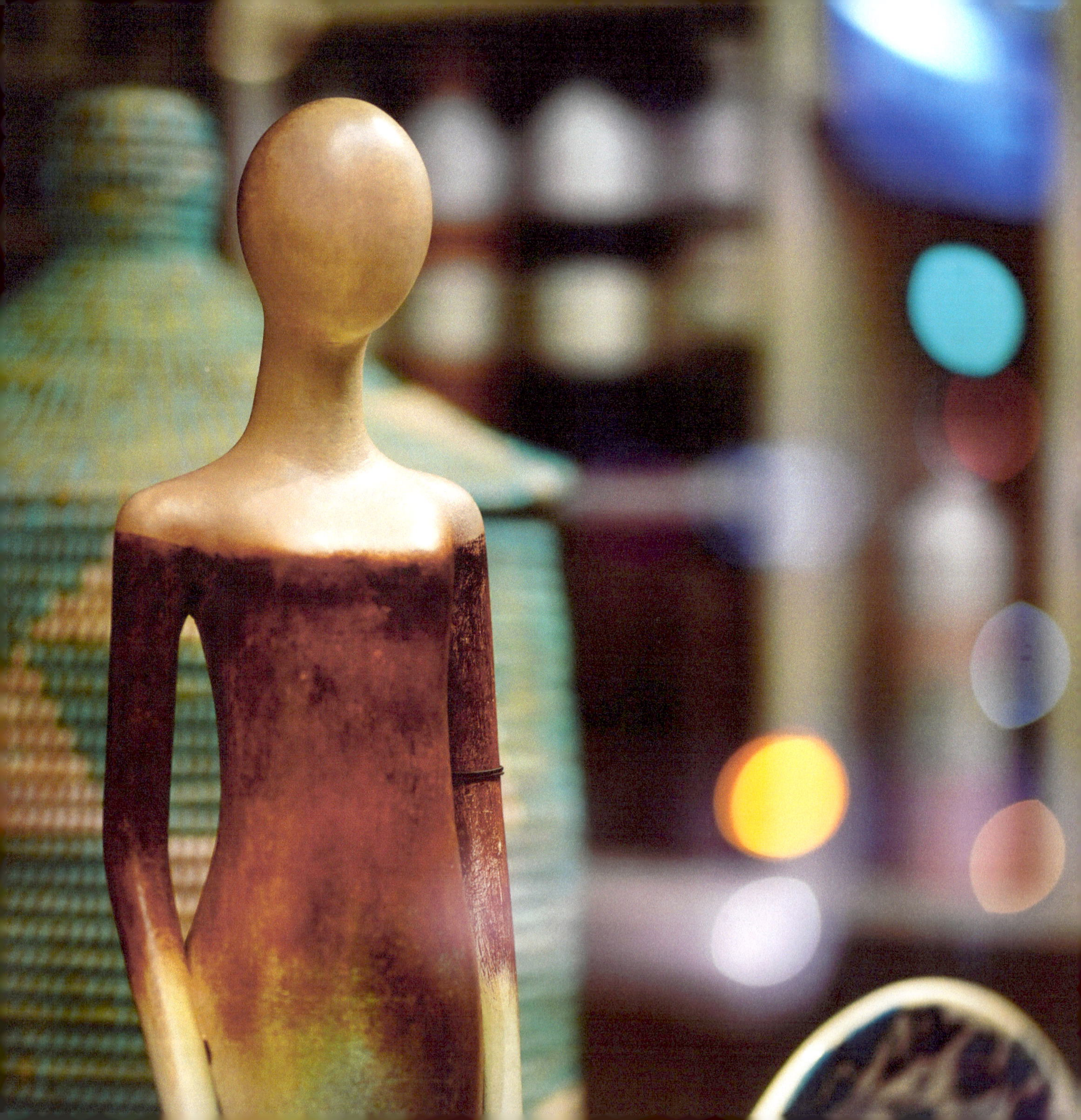

Complementarity

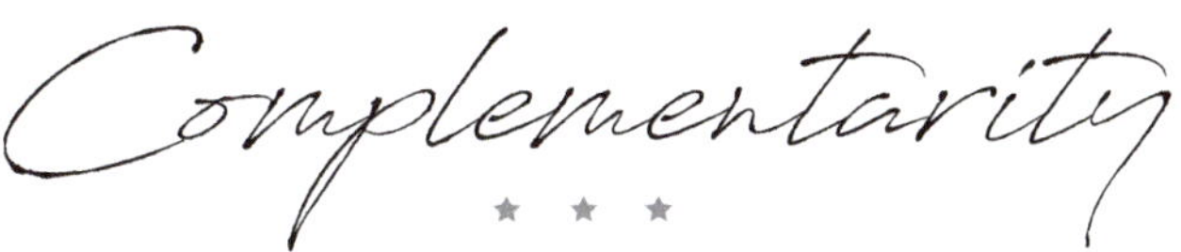

★ ★ ★

If people are nice to you, you'll be open to what they have to say.
If they aren't nice to you, you won't.

Prayer & Contemplation

Spirit of wisdom, protect me from being misled by those whose words are full of flattery, familiarity, and false promises, and keep me humble enough to learn from those whom I am tempted to dismiss as strange, difficult, or unfriendly. Even if others do not at fist show curiosity or respect regarding my viewpoints, help me show curiosity and respect regarding theirs.

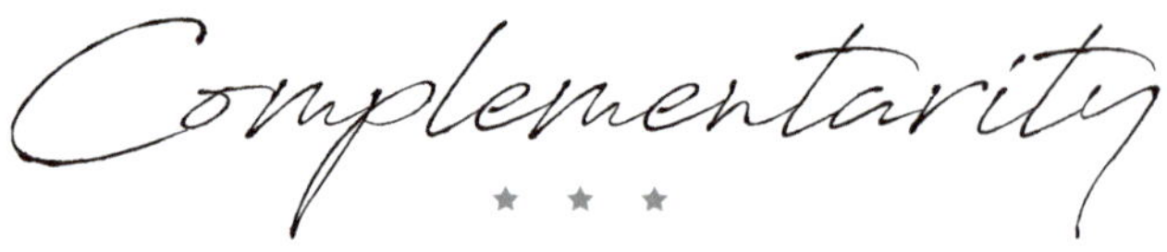

Complementarity

★ ★ ★

If people are nice to you, you'll be open to what they have to say.
If they aren't nice to you, you won't.

Complementarity

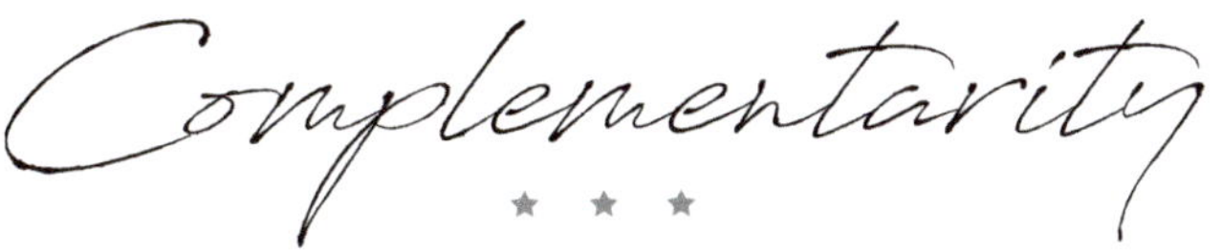

***

If people are nice to you, you'll be open to what they have to say.
If they aren't nice to you, you won't.

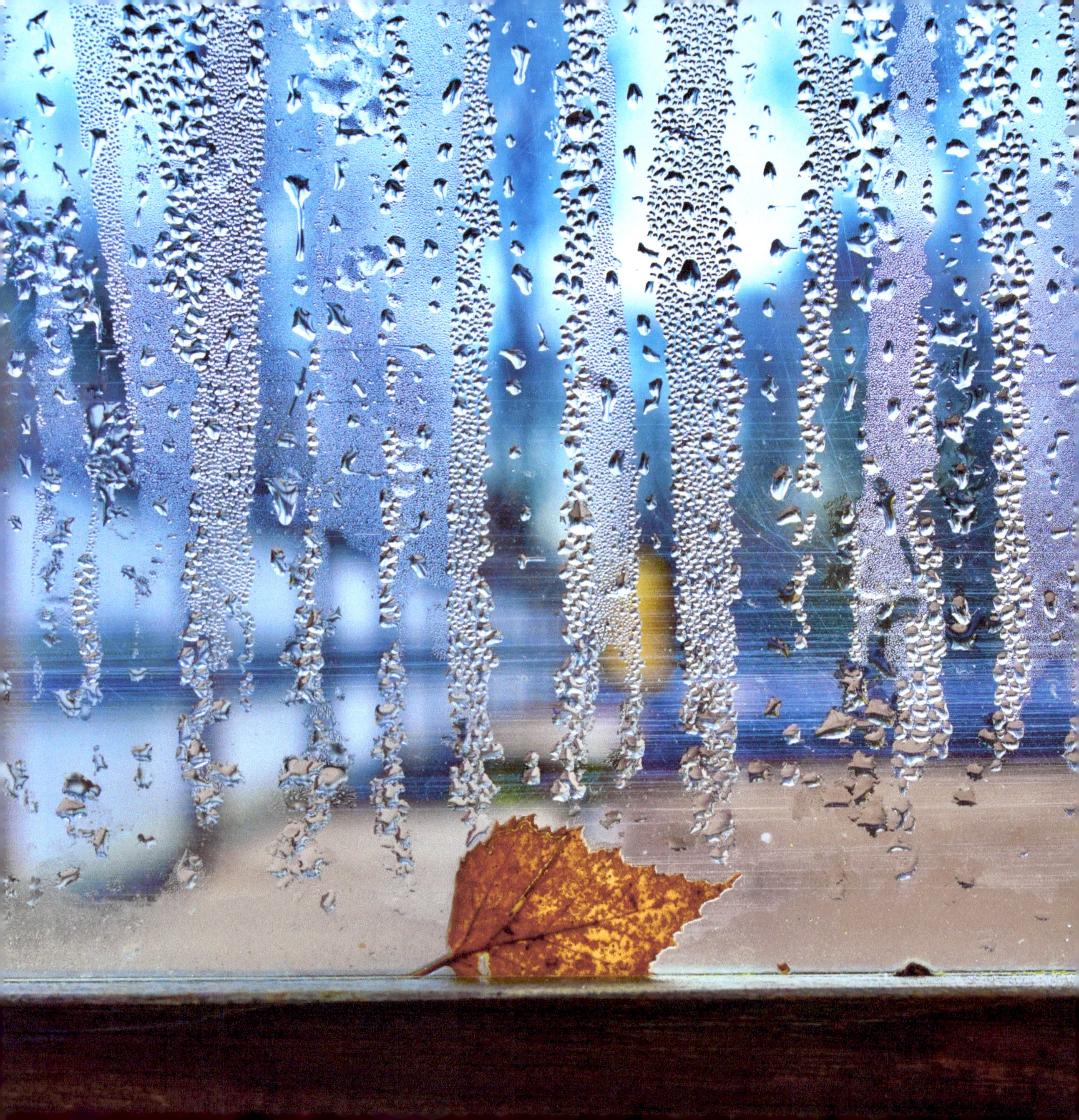

Contact

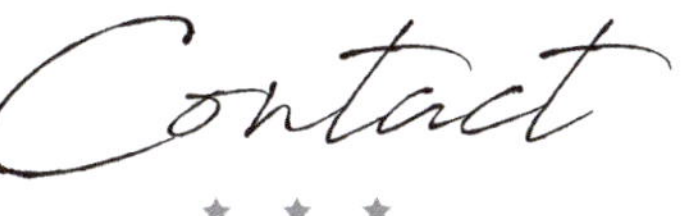

* * *

If you lack contact with someone, you won't see what they see.

Prayer & Contemplation

Revealer of insight, do not let me be satisfied to see only what is visible from my limited perspective. Grant me insatiable curiosity to understand what others can see from their diverse vantage points. Help me draw near to them, to walk with them, to see through their eyes, hear through their ears, and feel through their experience, so my horizons will be broadened through empathy.

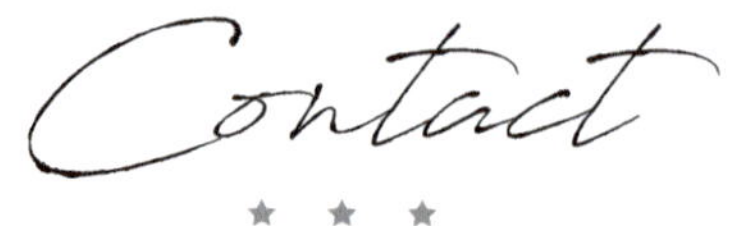

Contact

If you lack contact with someone, you won't see what they see.

Contact

★ ★ ★

If you lack contact with someone, you won't see what they see.

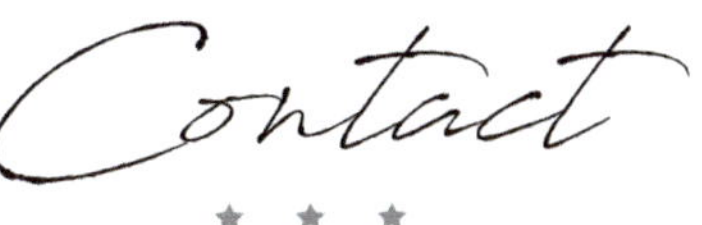

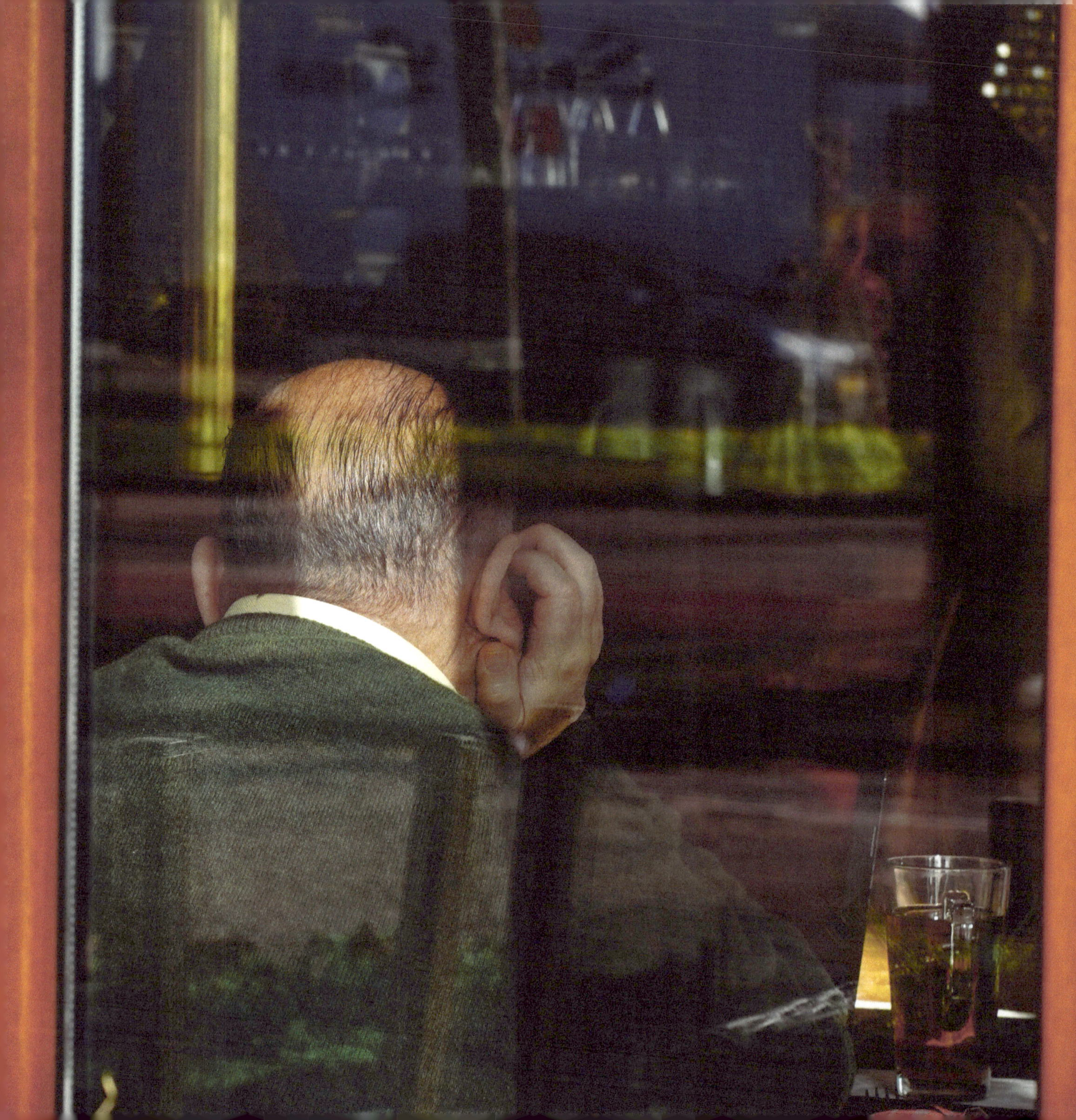

Conservative / Liberal

★ ★ ★

Our brains like to see as our party sees, and we flock with those who see as we do. Liberals see through a **nurturing parent** window, and Conservatives see through a **strict father** window. Liberals value moral arguments based on justice and compassion; conservatives also place a high value on arguments based on purity, loyalty, authority, and tradition.

....

....

....

....

....

....

....

Prayer & Contemplation

Holy Source of both surprise and consistency, help me never to be held captive by rigid ideology on the one had or addiction to novelty on the other. Do not let me be blinded by conformity or loyalty to any political party or economic theory. Help me always to do justice persistently, love kindness cheerfully, and with unflagging sincerity, to walk in humility with you, living God.

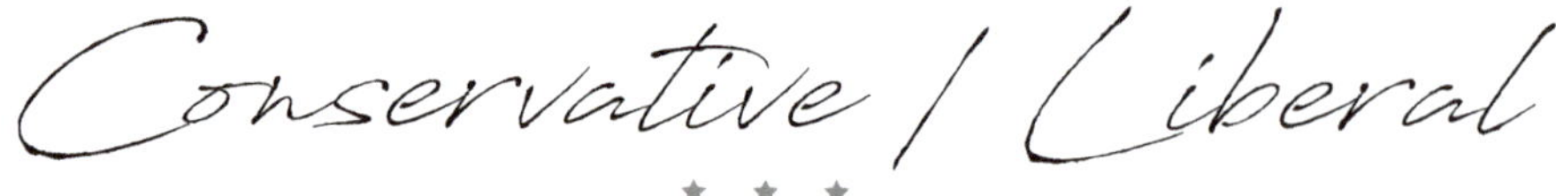

Conservative / Liberal

★ ★ ★

Our brains like to see as our party sees, and we flock with those who see as we do. Liberals see through a **nurturing parent** window, and Conservatives see through a **strict father** window. Liberals value moral arguments based on justice and compassion; conservatives also place a high value on arguments based on purity, loyalty, authority, and tradition.

Conservative / Liberal

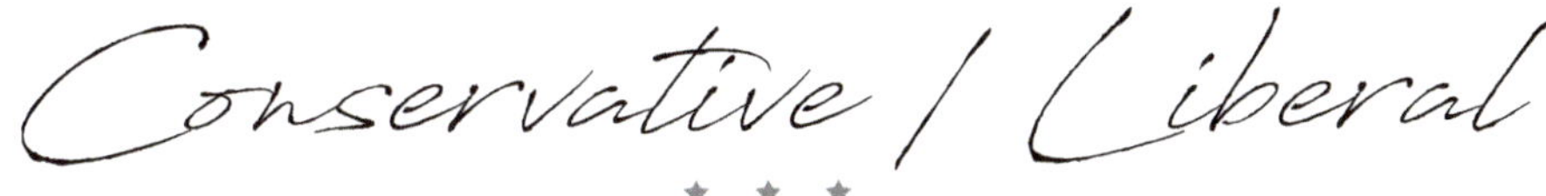

★ ★ ★

Our brains like to see as our party sees, and we flock with those who see as we do. Liberals see through a **nurturing parent** window, and Conservatives see through a **strict father** window. Liberals value moral arguments based on justice and compassion; conservatives also place a high value on arguments based on purity, loyalty, authority, and tradition.

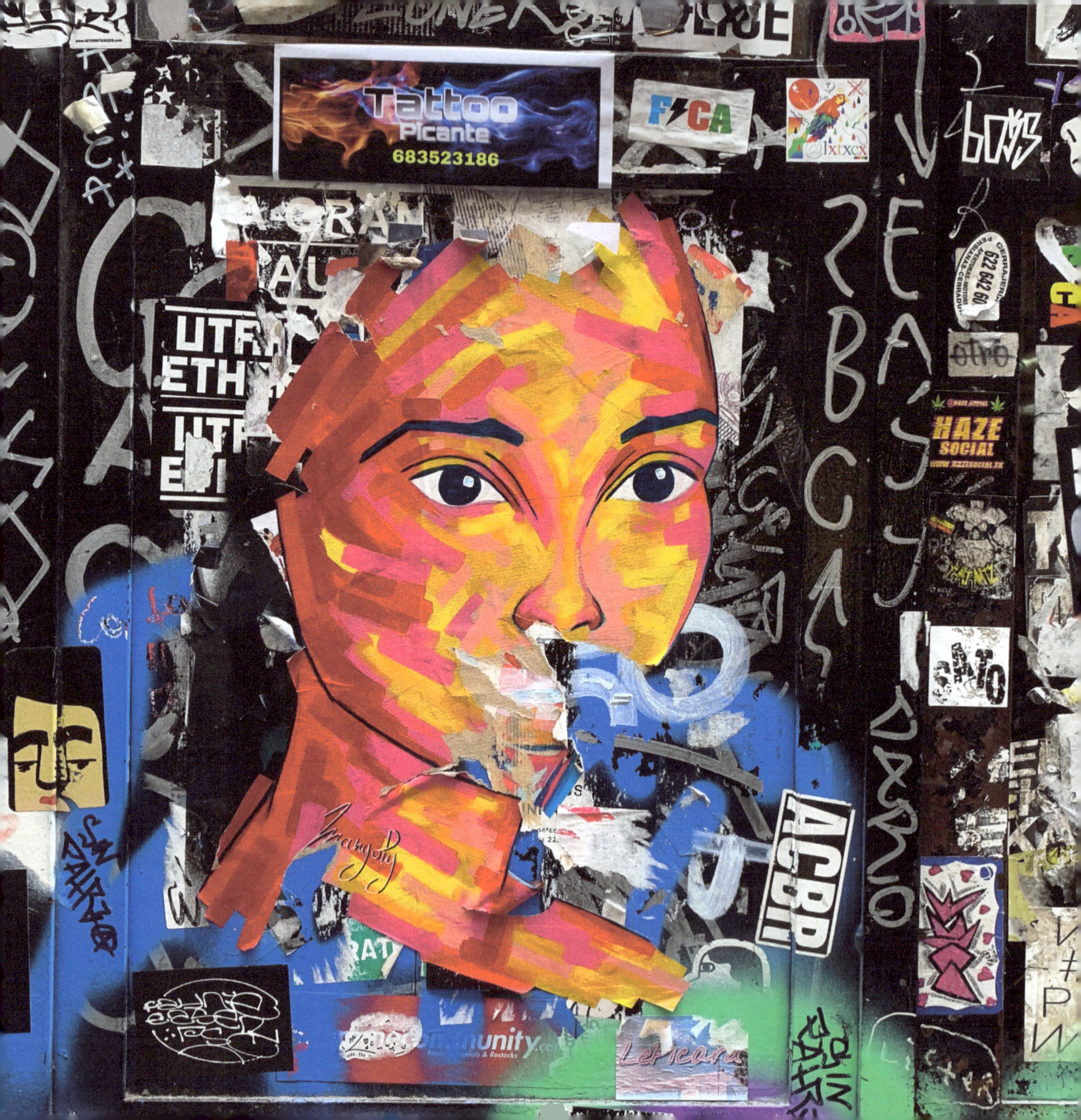

Tattoo
Picante
683523186
F*CA
@1x1xcx
boss
UTR
ETH
LITE
ED
HAZE
SOCIAL
WWW.HAZESOCIAL.TK
otro
622 642 60
CERRAJERÍA
SNO
ACBD
ACBD
Leticara
community.com

Consciousness

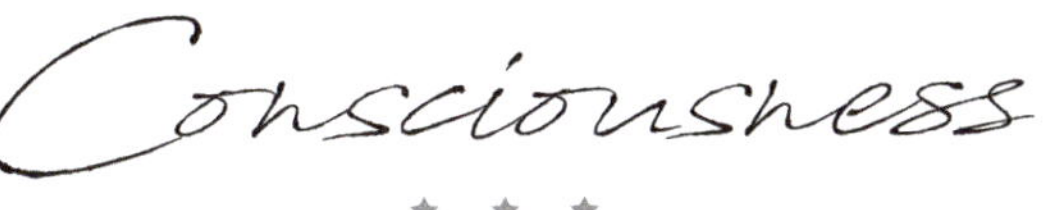

★ ★ ★

Our brains see from a location. A person's level of consciousness makes seeing some things possible and others impossible.

....

....

....

....

....

....

....

....

Prayer & Contemplation

Voice who beckons me toward growth, help me see what I am mature enough to see right now, and not only that: help me to know now how little I can know until I grow more mature. Grant me curiosity and awe to ever grow from strength to greater strength, so that I may honor the bottomless, limitless wonder, and the beauty, glory, and mystery that permeate this world.

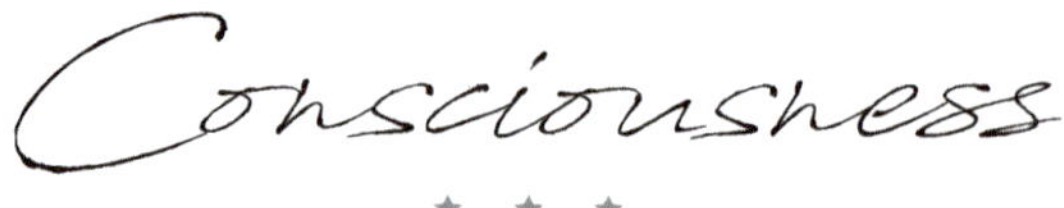

★ ★ ★

Our brains see from a location. A person's level of consciousness makes seeing some things possible and others impossible.

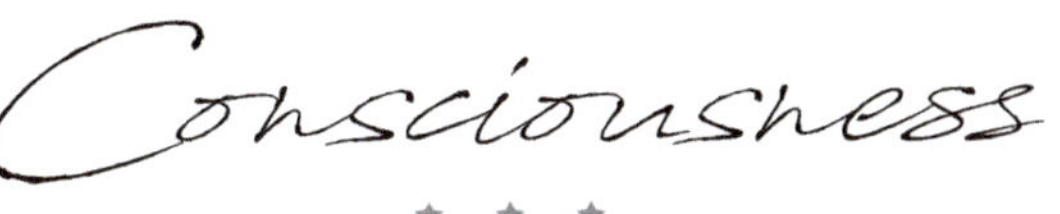

Consciousness

★ ★ ★

Our brains see from a location. A person's level of consciousness
makes seeing some things possible and others impossible.

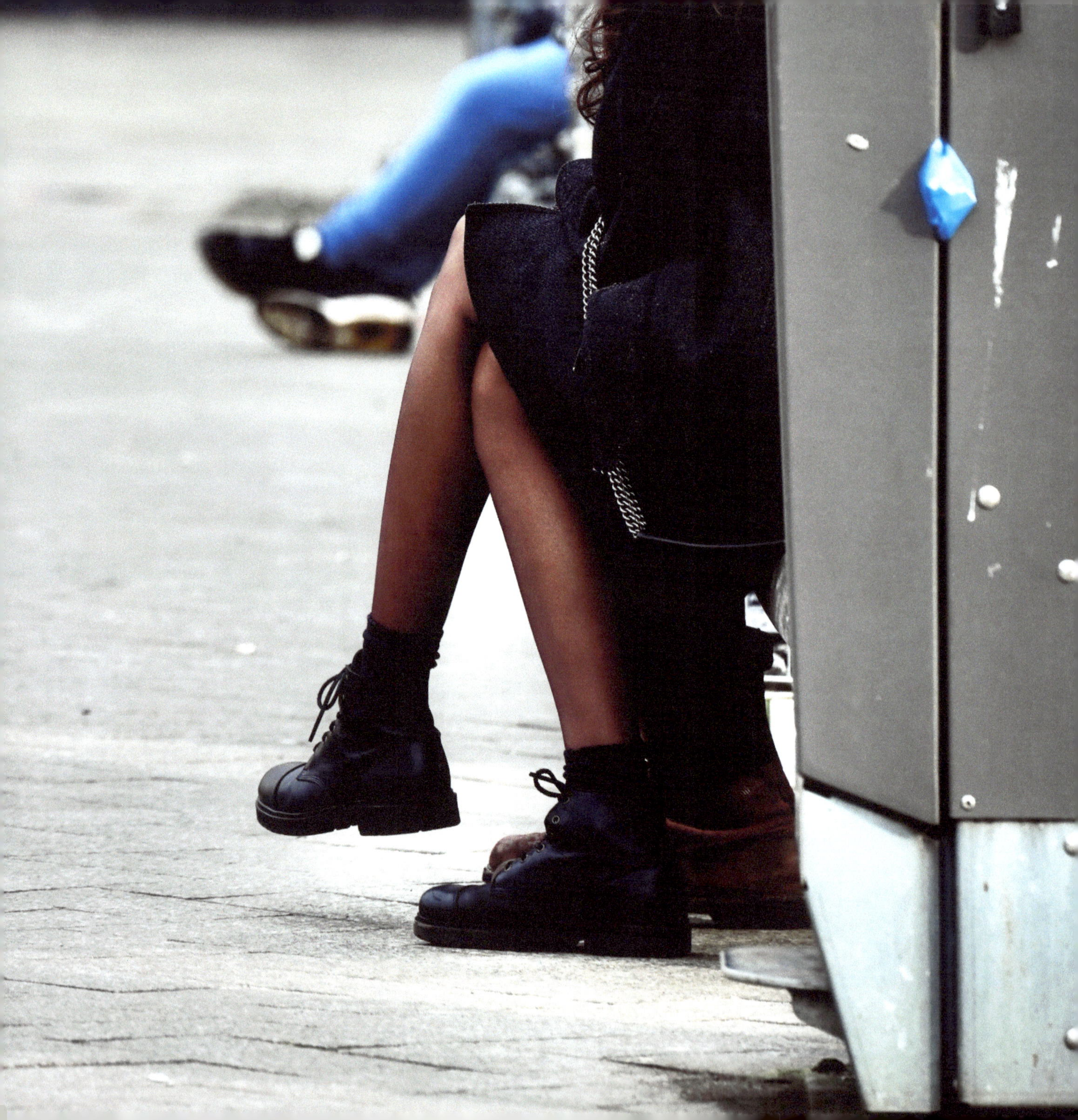

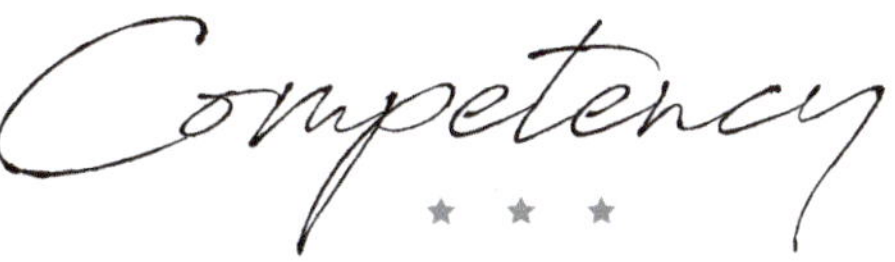

Competency

★ ★ ★

Our brains prefer to think of ourselves as above average. As a result,
we are incompetent at knowing how incompetent or competent
we are, so we may see less or more than we think..

....

....

....

....

....

....

....

Prayer & Contemplation

*Wellspring of all self-knowledge, give me humility and wisdom so that I do not overestimate
or underestimate my current level of competence. Please grant me a clear eye and sound
mind so I can assess myself, my abilities, and my limitations accurately, so that I will feel and
know when to speak up to teach and when to remain silent to learn.*

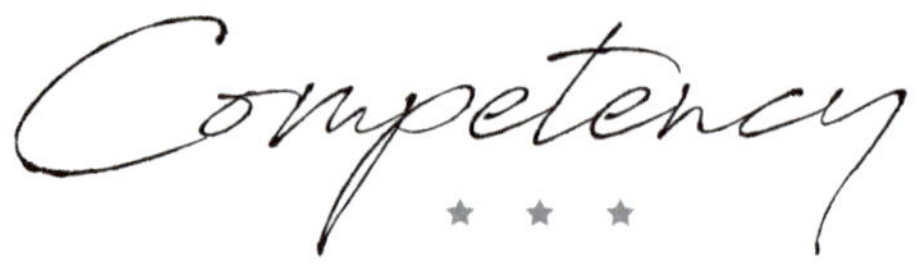

Competency

★ ★ ★

Our brains prefer to think of ourselves as above average. As a result,
we are incompetent at knowing how incompetent or competent
we are, so we may see less or more than we think..

Competency

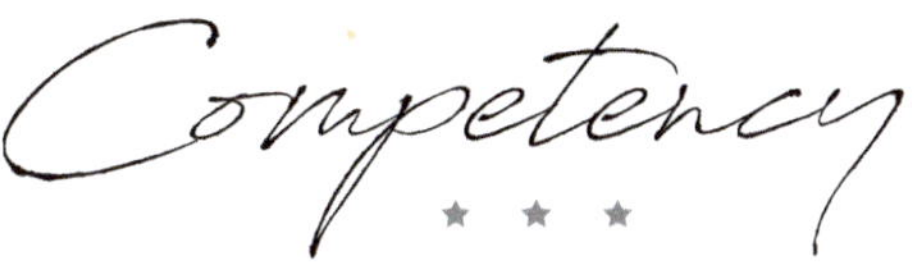

Our brains prefer to think of ourselves as above average. As a result,
we are incompetent at knowing how incompetent or competent
we are, so we may see less or more than we think..

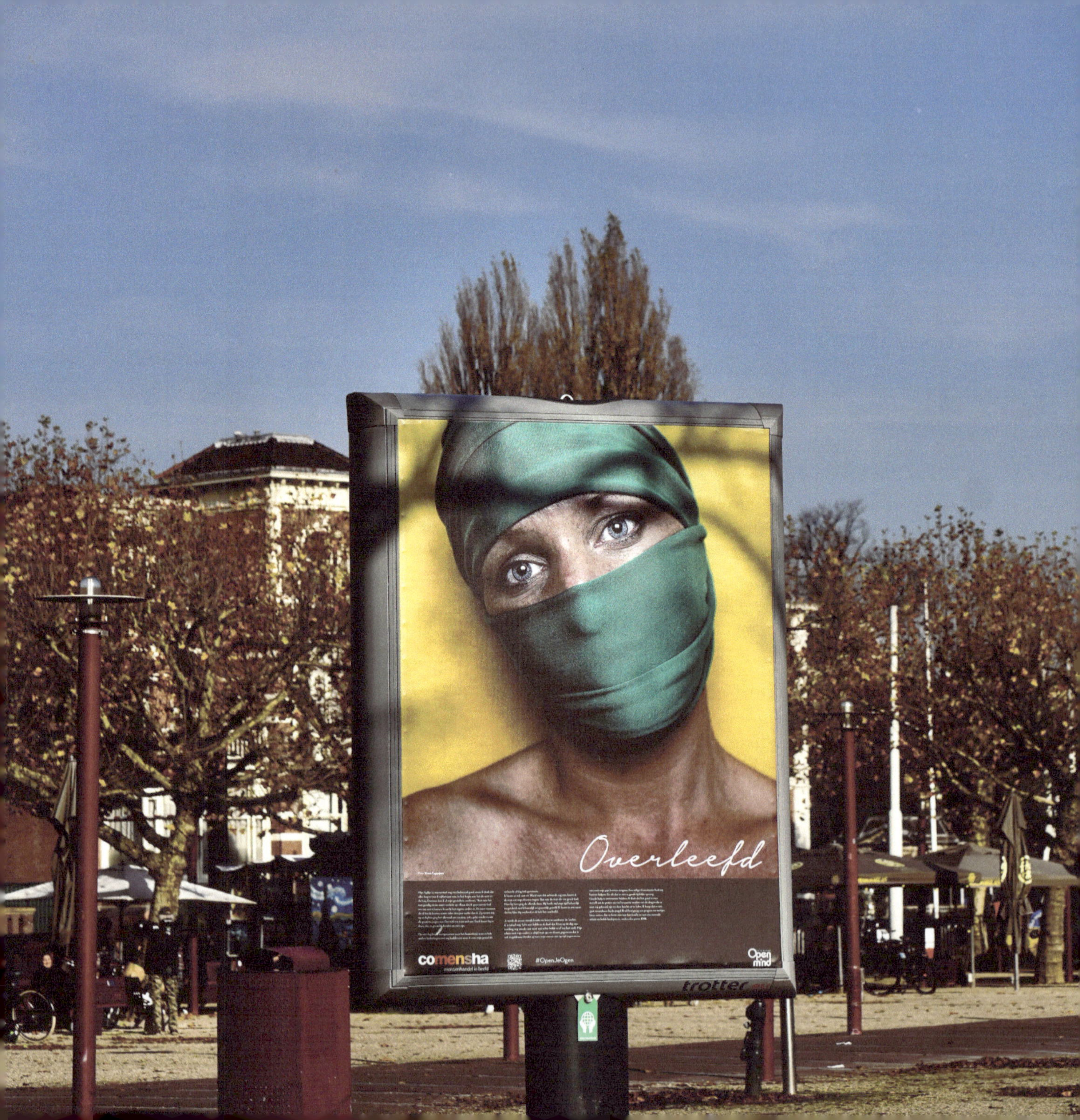

Overleefd
comensha
mensenhandel in beeld
#OpenJeOgen
Open mind
trotter

Confidence

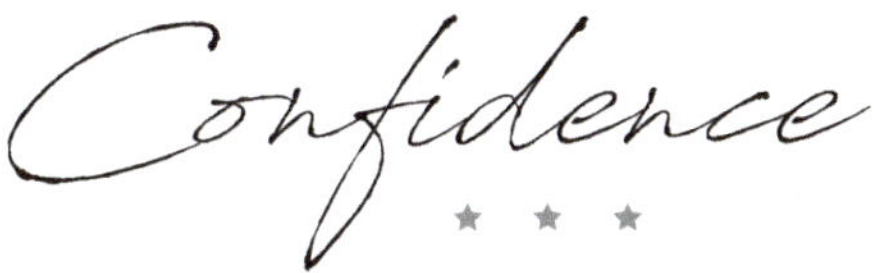

★ ★ ★

Our brains prefer a confident lie to a hesitant truth. We mistake confidence for competence, and we are all vulnerable to the lies of confident people.

....

....

....

....

....

....

....

....

Prayer & Contemplation

Cosmic witness who cannot lie, keep me vigilant against con artists for whom lies and truth are spoken with equal confidence, and who tell me what I want to hear so that I will do what they desire. Protect me from surrendering to others my responsibility to think for myself.

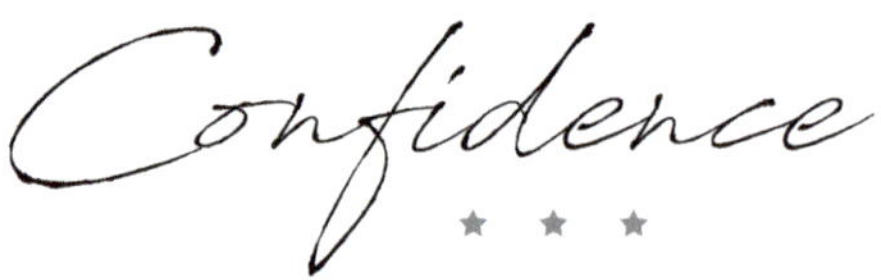

Confidence

Our brains prefer a confident lie to a hesitant truth. We mistake confidence for competence, and we are all vulnerable to the lies of confident people.

Confidence

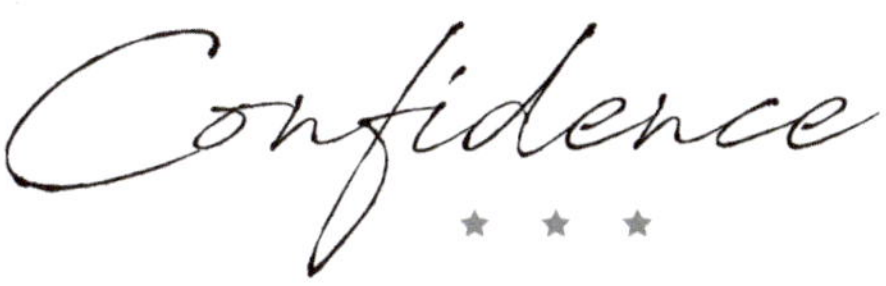

★ ★ ★

Our brains prefer a confident lie to a hesitant truth. We mistake confidence for competence, and we are all vulnerable to the lies of confident people.

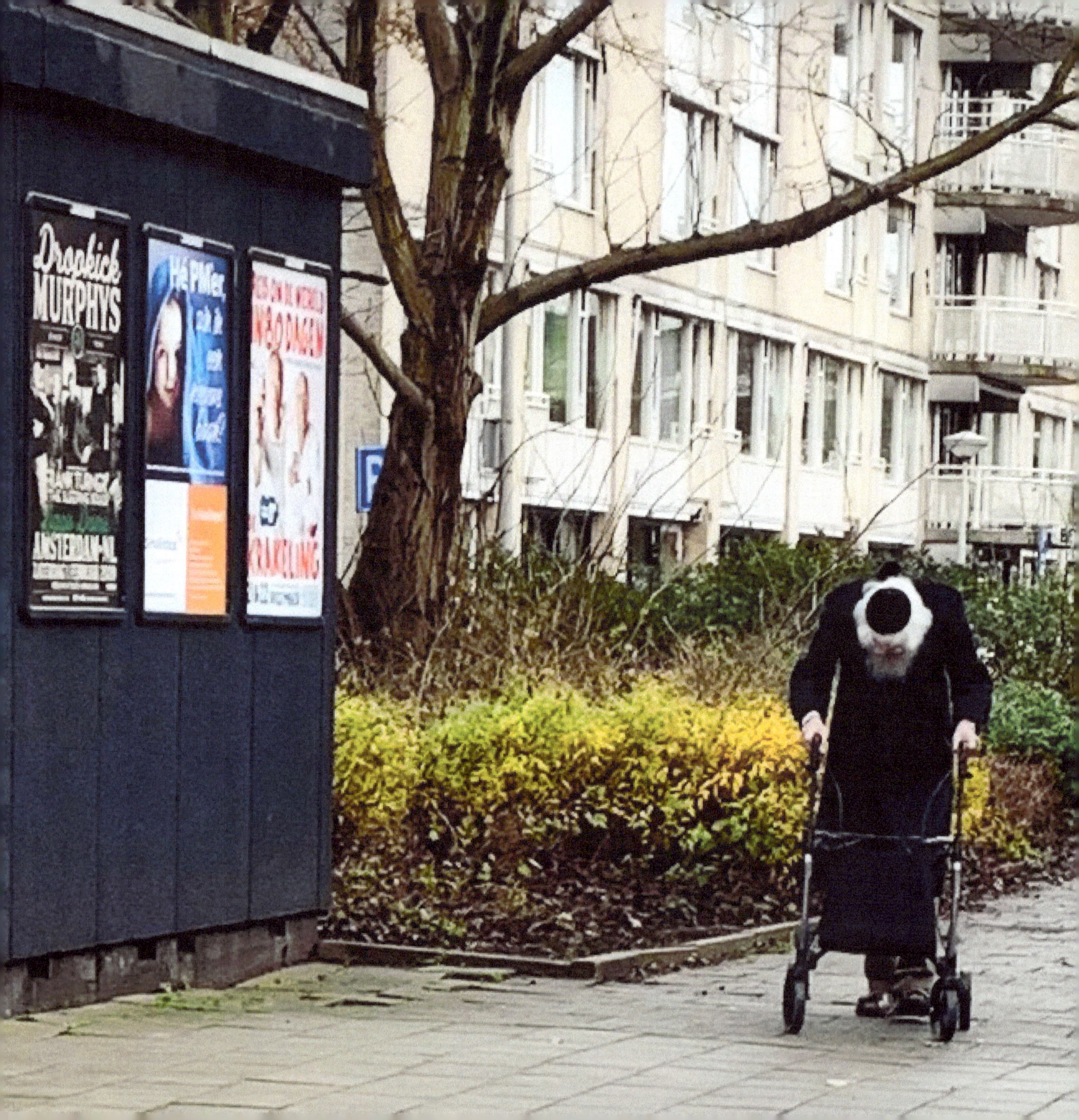
Dropkick
MURPHYS
AMSTERDAM-NL

Conspiracy

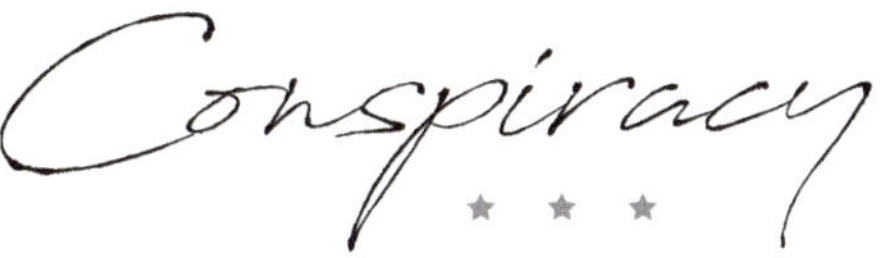

★ ★ ★

....

....

....

....

....

....

....

....

Prayer & Contemplation

*Companion who walks with me in light and darkness, help me guard my heart from stories
and theories that cast me as an innocent victim or virtuous hero, while simultaneously casting
someone else as villain or enemy. Instead, help me join your cosmic conspiracy of kindness,
justice, joy, and peace for all, seeing myself and all my neighbors as equal beneficiaries of
your boundless, merciful love.*

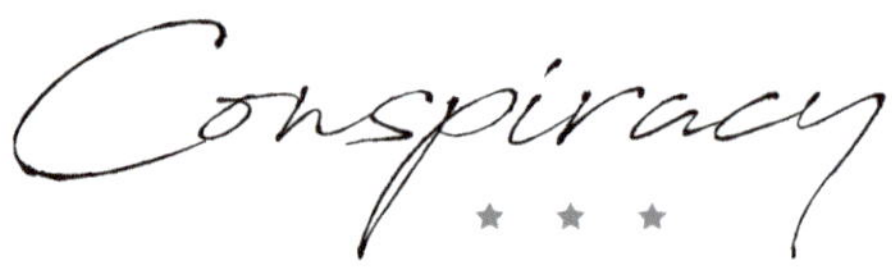

Conspiracy

★ ★ ★

When we feel shame, we are vulnerable to stories that cast us as the victims of an evil conspiracy by some enemy "other." Our brains like stories in which we're either the hero or the victim . . . never the villain.

Conspiracy

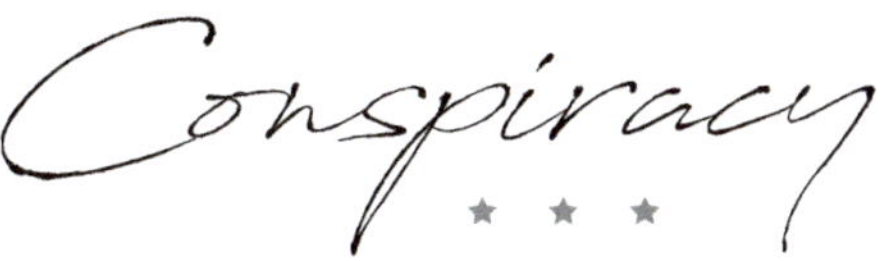

★ ★ ★

When we feel shame, we are vulnerable to stories that cast us as the victims of an evil conspiracy by some enemy "other." Our brains like stories in which we're either the hero or the victim . . . never the villain.

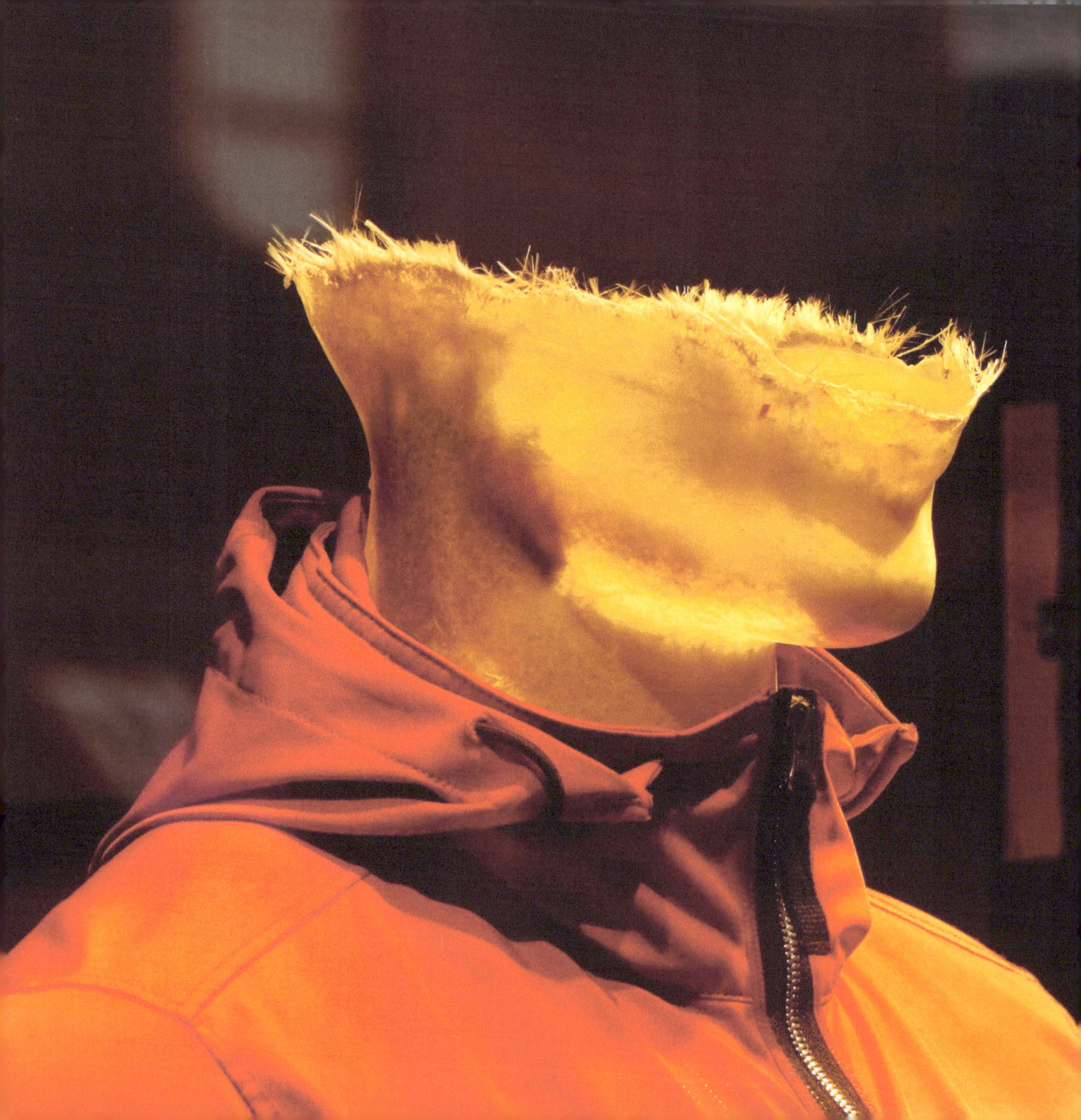

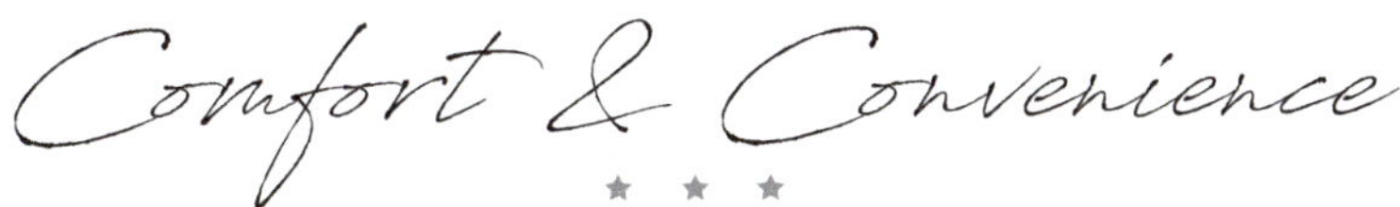

Comfort & Convenience

★ ★ ★

Our brains welcome data that allows us to relax and be happy and reject data
that requires us to adjust, work, or inconvenience ourselves.

....

....

....

....

....

....

....

Prayer & Contemplation

Spirit of truth who sets us free by the truth, please strengthen my desire for truth, so that I will face rather than reject truths that will inconvenience me. Grant me resolve to welcome the pain that often comes with wisdom. Help me choose empathy over apathy. Help me choose courage over complacency. And help me to abhor the bliss that accompanies ignorance.

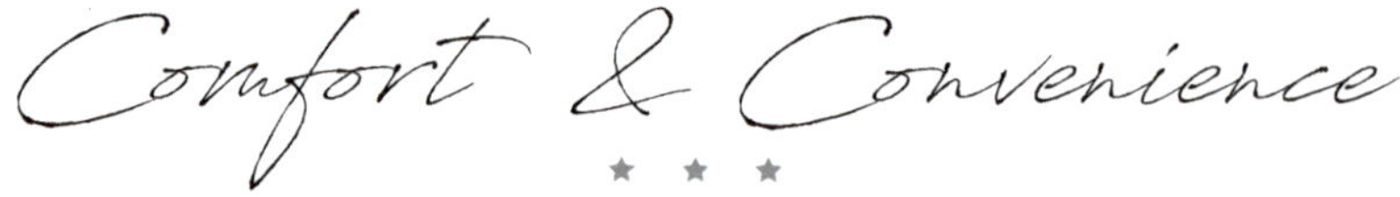

Our brains welcome data that allows us to relax and be happy and reject data that requires us to adjust, work, or inconvenience ourselves.

Comfort & Convenience

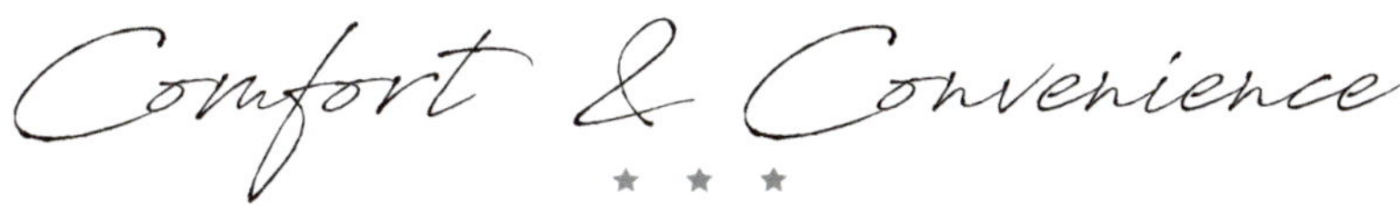

* ★ ★ ★ *

Our brains welcome data that allows us to relax and be happy and reject data
that requires us to adjust, work, or inconvenience ourselves.

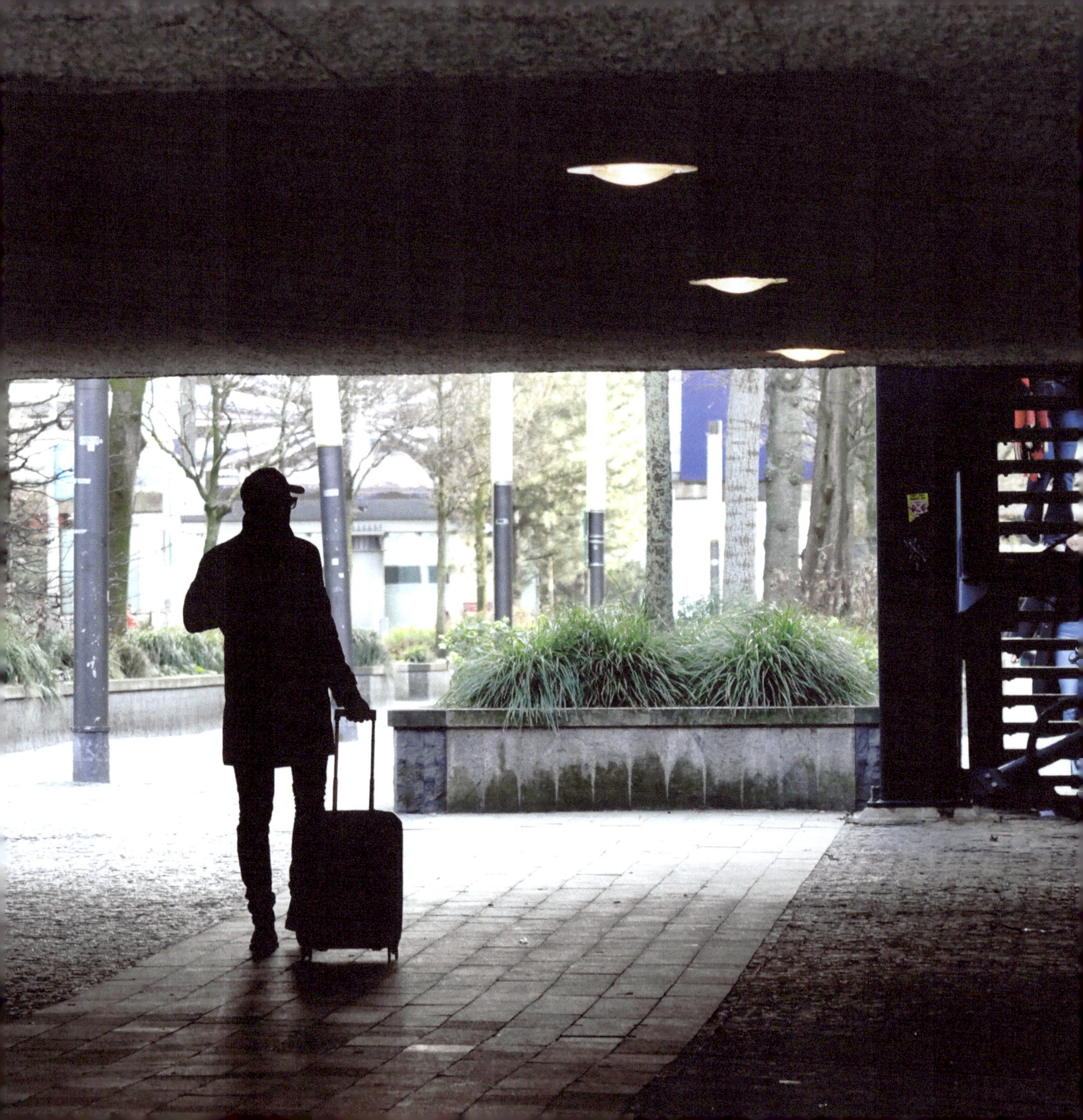

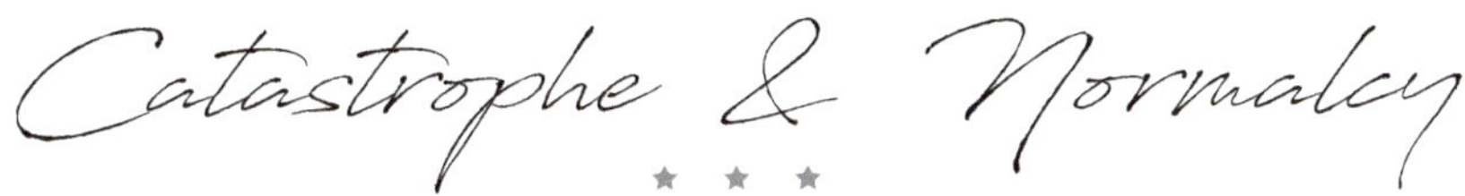

Catastrophe & Normalcy

★ ★ ★

Our brains are wired to set a baseline of normalcy and assume what feels normal has always been and will always remain. As a result, we minimize threats and are vulnerable to disasters, especially ones that develop slowly.

....

....

....

....

....

....

....

....

Prayer & Contemplation

Holy Light who illumines what is real, help me to see danger that is all the more threatening because it unfolds gradually, and likewise, help me to see possibility that is easily missed because it emerges slowly and subtly. Grant me, I pray, the long view..

Catastrophe & Normalcy

★ ★ ★

Our brains are wired to set a baseline of normalcy and assume what feels normal has always been and will always remain. As a result, we minimize threats and are vulnerable to disasters, especially ones that develop slowly.

Catastrophe & Normalcy

★ ★ ★

Our brains are wired to set a baseline of normalcy and assume what feels normal has always been and will always remain. As a result, we minimize threats and are vulnerable to disasters, especially ones that develop slowly.

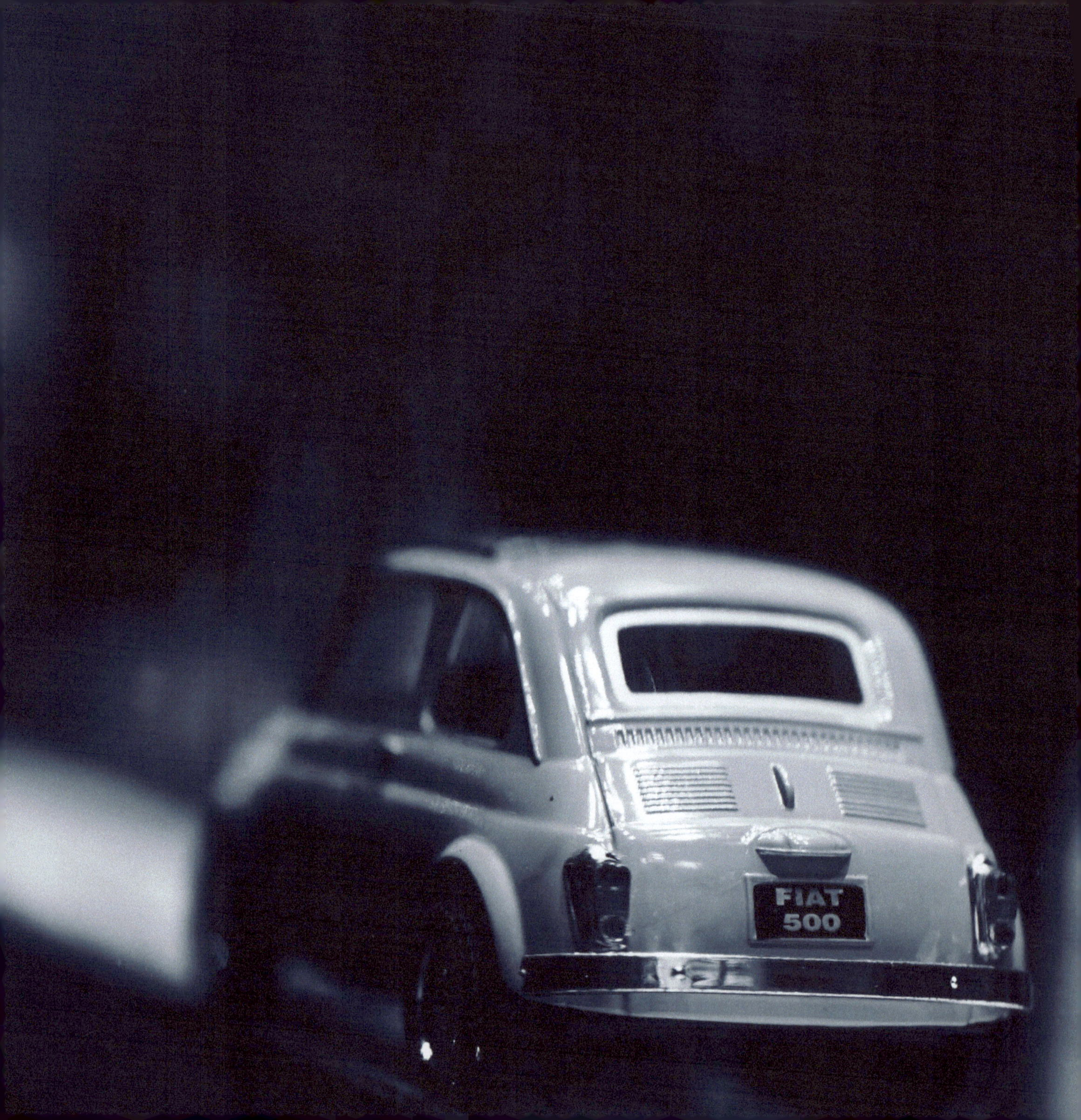

FIAT
500

Cash

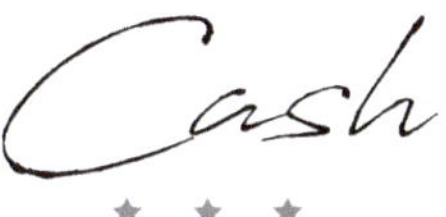

★ ★ ★

Our brains are wired to see within the framework of our economy, and we see what helps us make money. It is very hard to see anything that interferes with our way of making a living.

....

....

....

....

....

....

....

....

Prayer & Contemplation

Beloved One who loves me, help me to hate money in comparison with you, and help me see in the love of money the hidden root of all kinds of evil, so that I may see and cherish what has true value, freely giving what I cannot keep to gain what I cannot lose.

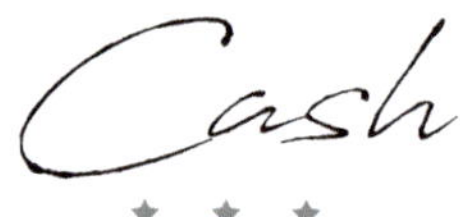

Our brains are wired to see within the framework of our economy, and we see what helps us make money. It is very hard to see anything that interferes with our way of making a living.

Cash

★ ★ ★

Our brains are wired to see within the framework of our economy, and we see what helps us make money. It is very hard to see anything that interferes with our way of making a living.

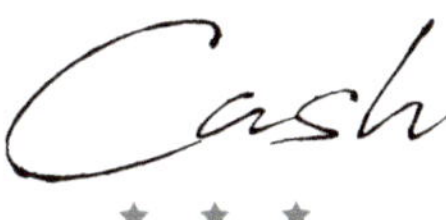

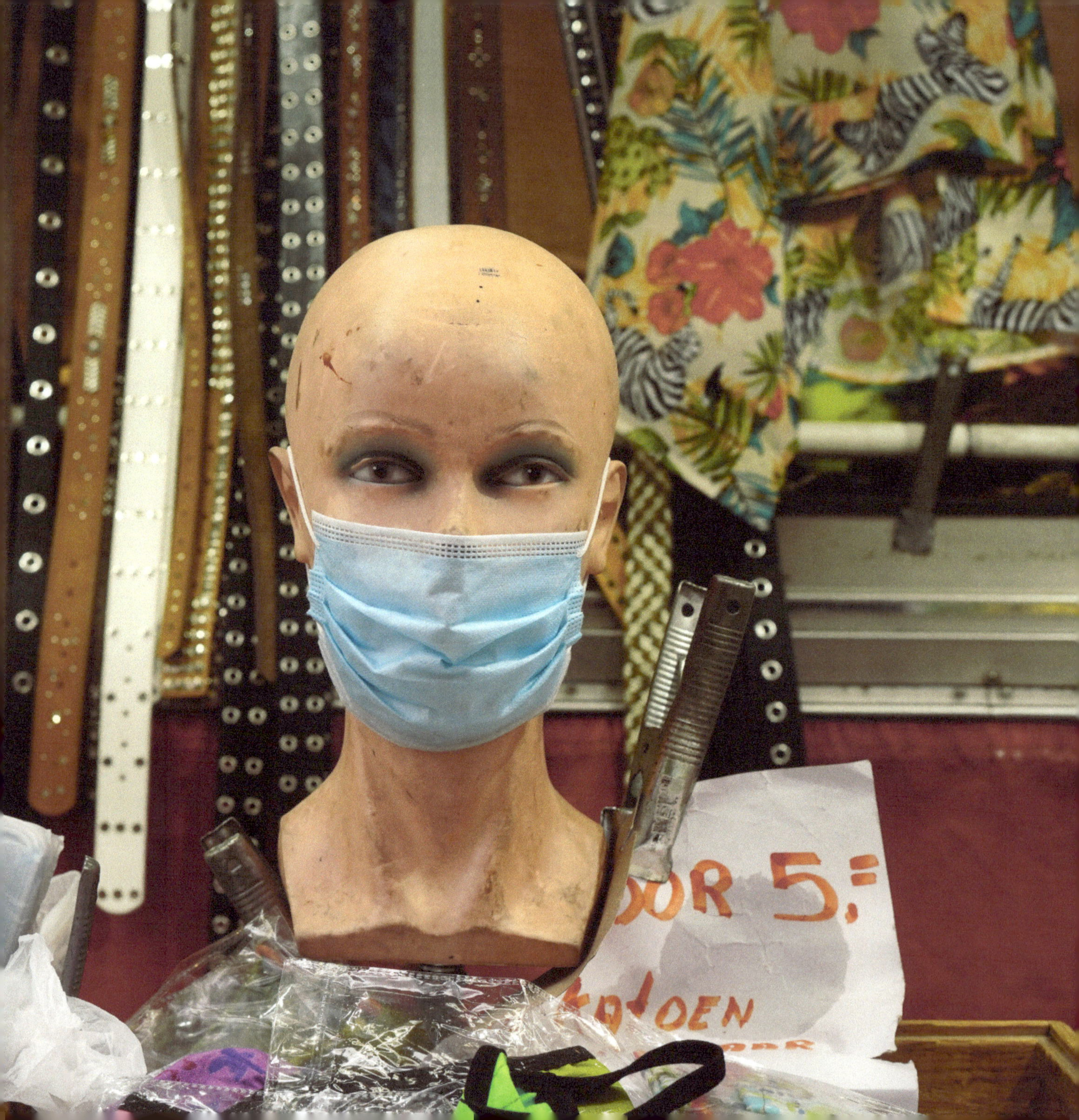
OOR 5,=
KOJDEN

Closing Prayer

* * *

Source of Wonder, *help us see with wonder.*

Depth of Mystery, *help us find delight in truths so profound that they surpass all knowing.*

Fountain of Compassion, *help us see with compassion.*

Bringer of Justice, *help us see with justice.*

Revealer of Truth, *help us see what is real.*

Holy Wisdom *whose presence fills our ever-expanding universe, help our horizons ever to expand.*

Light of Glory, *help us to see with humility and awe.*

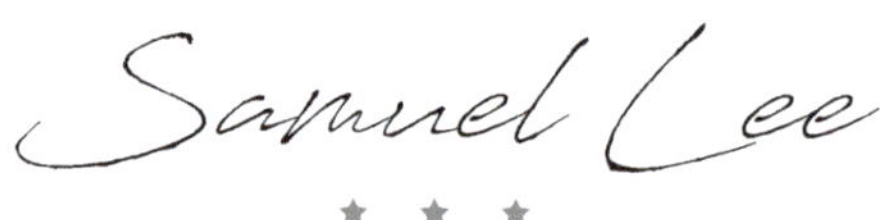

★ ★ ★

Samuel Lee is a Christian theologian, sociologist, and human rights advocate from the Netherlands. He was named **Theologian of the Year** in the Netherlands in 2019. For his dedication to social justice, he was knighted in the **Order of Oranje Nassau** in 2020.

Sam is also the founder and president of the **Foundation Academy of Amsterdam**, which provides academic education to migrants and refugees and the director of the **Center for Theology of Migration** at **VU University's Faculty of Religion and Theology**, where he lectures **Theology of Migration**.

Sam senses God's heartbeat in the smallest details, the unspoken whispers, and the most unexpected places . . . his "eye on the unseen" makes Sam a wonder and passionate street photographer.

Brian & Samuel have been friends for many years.

Brian D. McLaren

★ ★ ★

Brian is an author, speaker, activist, and public theologian. A former college English teacher and pastor, he is a passionate advocate for "a new kind of Christianity" – just, generous, and working with people of all faiths for the common good.

He is a faculty member of **The Living School** and podcaster with **Learning How to See**, which are part of the **Center for Action and Contemplation**. He is also an **Auburn Senior Fellow** and works closely with the **Wild Goose Festival,** the **Fair Food Program, Vote Common Good,** and **Progressive Christianity**.

His recent projects include an illustrated children's book (for all ages) called **Cory and the Seventh Story** and **The Galapagos Islands: A Spiritual Journey.**

His newest book is **Faith After Doubt** (January 2021), and his next release, **Do I Stay Christian?** will be available Spring 2022.

We trust this journal will be useful to you, to be used alone or in conjunction with the e-book or the podcast. _See below._

For more information see **brianmclaren.net**

★ ★ ★

Why Don't They Get It? Overcoming Bias in Others - and Yourself
brianmclaren.net/store

Learning How To See
cac.org/podcast/learning-how-to-see

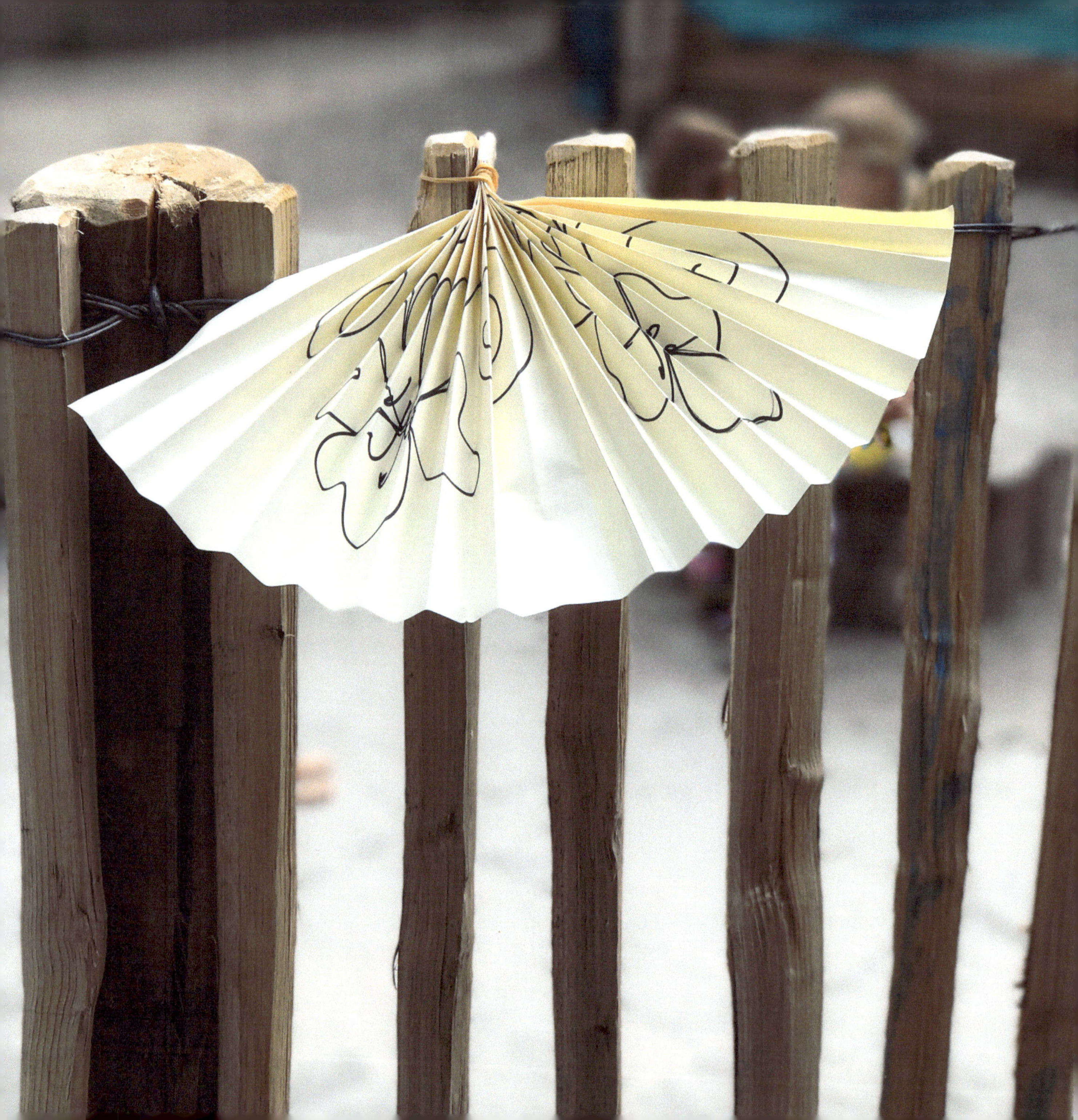

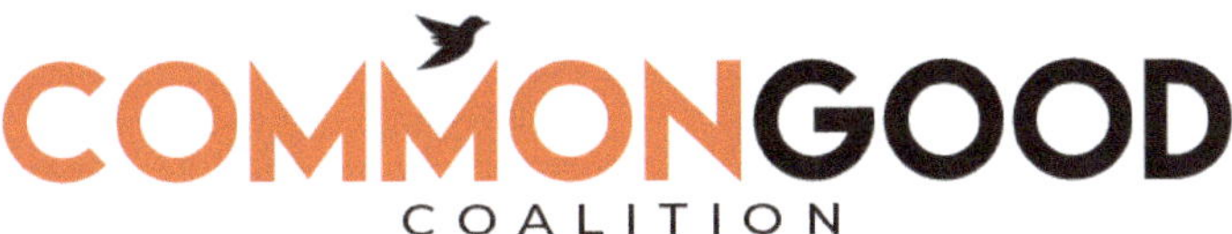

* * *

As a community of seekers, leaders, artists, poets we are always in search of ways to live our lives for the common good. We understand that what is good for others is ultimately good for us as well.

We invite you to join us in this journey … a path toward discovering how we measure the values and focus of our lives, our work, our play and our faith by the **common good**.

cgcoalition.com

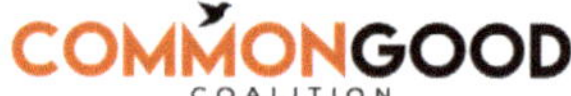